Beagles

Stephanie Finne

Checkerboard
Library

An Imprint of Abdo Publishing
www.abdopublishing.com

www.abdopublishing.com

Published by Abdo Publishing, a division of ABDO, PO Box 398166, Minneapolis, MN 55439.
Copyright © 2015 by Abdo Consulting Group, Inc. International copyrights reserved in all
countries. No part of this book may be reproduced in any form without written permission from
the publisher. Checkerboard Library™ is a trademark and logo of Abdo Publishing.

Printed in the United States of America, North Mankato, Minnesota.
102014
012015

Cover Photo: iStockphoto
Interior Photos: Alamy p. 7; Glow Images p. 21; iStockphoto pp. 1, 5, 9, 11, 13, 15, 16–17, 18–19

Series Coordinator: Tamara L. Britton
Editors: Megan M. Gunderson, Bridget O'Brien
Production: Jillian O'Brien

Library of Congress Cataloging-in-Publication Data

Finne, Stephanie, author.
  Beagles / Stephanie Finne.
      pages cm. -- (Dogs)
  Audience: Ages 8-12.
  Includes index.
  ISBN 978-1-62403-672-9
  1. Beagle (Dog breed)--Juvenile literature. I. Title.
  SF429.B3F56 2015
  636.753'7--dc23
                            2014025404

Contents

The Dog Family

Dogs come in many shapes and sizes. Yet, all of these dogs belong to the family **Canidae**. The name comes from the Latin word for "dog," which is *canis*.

For more than 12,000 years, dogs and humans have lived and worked together. Early humans adopted gray wolf pups. They trained the pups to be hunting dogs. These wolves are the ancestors of modern dogs.

Over time, humans began **breeding** dogs for other activities. Today, there are more than 400 breeds. One of these is the beagle. Beagles are members of the hound group. Like the first dogs, beagles are hunting dogs.

The beagle

Beagles

Early beagles assisted English gentlemen with hunting rabbits. These dogs were not called beagles until 1475. Originally, there were rough-coated and smooth-coated beagles. And, the size of the dogs varied greatly.

After the American **Civil War**, American **breeders** began to import beagles from England. They began to create a standard beagle type.

In 1884, the **American Kennel Club (AKC)** and the American-English Beagle Club were formed. The American-English Beagle Club set the breed standard for American beagles. Beagles were accepted into the AKC in 1885.

In 1888, the National Beagle Club (NBC) was formed to hold field trials. Club leaders hoped to

Beagles are still used for hunting today.

improve the **breed**'s hunting qualities. The American-English Beagle Club soon **merged** with the NBC. Today, the beagle is the fourth most popular breed in the United States.

What They're Like

Beagles are scent hounds. Their instincts are to hunt small game. They have an excellent sense of smell. So, don't be surprised if they run off to follow a scent!

Beagles have a merry disposition. They are always ready to join in an adventure! But they are also independent. It can be difficult to keep them focused on training. Exercise will burn off some of their energy and allow for better focus.

These smart, curious dogs are pack animals. They prefer to be with their families for most of the day. If they are unsupervised for longer than four hours a day, they can get into trouble. This includes a lot of barking and howling!

Beagles love people and being the center of attention. They are friendly with other dogs and humans. A beagle can be a wonderful addition to your family.

This beagle's tail pointing up and nose pointing out indicate he has scented game.

Coat and Color

Beagles have short, smooth coats. Like other hounds, they have a double coat. The outer coat is waterproof and protects beagles from weather and dirt. The **dense**, thick **undercoat** keeps them warm.

Beagles have the coloring of a true hound. This means they can be any combination of white, black, tan, **lemon**, blue-gray, or red-brown. However, most beagles have **tricolor** coats made of shades of black, white, and brown. Beagles have black noses and brown or **hazel** eyes.

Many beagles have freckles, called ticking. The freckles can be tan or black. They appear on the dog's legs, but can be on the body and tail as well.

The different coloring
and freckles on your
beagle mean you can
have a one-of-a-kind
best friend!

Size

Beagles are one of two sizes. They can be under 13 inches (33 cm) or between 13 and 15 inches (38 cm) tall. The smaller beagles are usually about 18 pounds (8 kg). The larger beagles are about 30 pounds (14 kg). These sturdy dogs are surprisingly heavy for their size. Males are heavier than females.

A beagle's head is round at the top. The medium-length **muzzle** ends with a nose that has wide nostrils for capturing scents. The beagle has big, round eyes. Its long, low-set ears can reach to the tip of the nose. The ears have a rounded tip.

This **breed**'s square, muscular body has a medium neck and short back. Short, muscular legs end in round, firm paws. The beagle's short tail is set high. It has a slight curve and greets everyone with happy wagging!

Beagles do not drool. And, they have no doggy odor!

Care

Beagles require regular visits with a veterinarian. The dog will receive needed **vaccines** at its visit. The vet can **spay** or **neuter** dogs that will not be **bred**.

Beagles are active dogs. They need two hours of exercise each day. Daily walks or active play is important for your beagle. Be sure to leash your dog! As a hunting dog, a beagle may follow a scent and ignore its owner's call. A fenced-in yard will keep your beagle safe.

The beagle's short coat **sheds** an average amount. A brushing once or twice a week will keep a beagle properly groomed. Grooming is a good time to check the dog's feet, ears, and eyes for problems. And don't forget to trim its toenails. Regularly brushing your dog's teeth will prevent tooth decay and gum disease.

Younger dogs can have annual checkups. Older dogs will need to be examined more often.

Beagles have a bold attitude and like to be part of a pack. They are happiest when they are with other pets or their families. The most important things you can provide for your beagle are companionship and love.

15

Feeding

A balanced diet and regular feeding times will keep your beagle healthy. Feeding a dog once or twice a day is most common. Many owners feed their adult dogs in the morning and in the evening. Puppies and older dogs may need a more frequent feeding schedule.

There are different types of dog food to choose from. A high-quality commercial dog food will provide the proper **nutrients**.

Dry foods help clean a dog's teeth. Semimoist foods are softer and do not need to be refrigerated. Canned foods are moist, but they spoil quickly. In addition to a healthy diet, your beagle will need fresh, clean water every day.

Beagles are known for their healthy appetites! It is important to watch how much your beagle eats. It can become overweight, which can lead to health problems. Beagles that hunt will need to eat more than pet beagles. Your veterinarian can recommend a feeding schedule to keep your dog's weight stable.

Beagles love food and are always in search of it. They have perfected the art of begging and will do anything to get a snack!

Things They Need

As you can see, food and water are important! Your beagle will need dishes from which to eat and drink. Both bowls should be kept clean. This will keep the dog from becoming sick by eating from dirty dishes and drinking stale water.

Your dog will need a few other things, too. A collar with an identification tag is a good start. A vet can also insert a **microchip** in your beagle. Both will help identify your pet if you lose track of each other.

After a busy day, your beagle will need a place to rest. A crate or a bed gives the dog its own place to call home.

Toys will give your beagle a way to burn off some energy.

Puppies

Like all dogs, a female beagle is **pregnant** for about 63 days after mating. Beagles usually have seven puppies in a **litter**. Puppies are born blind and deaf and they cannot walk.

After two weeks, a puppy's eyes will start to open. After four weeks, the puppy will be able to see, hear, and play. At two months old, the puppy is ready for some basic training.

Beagle puppies are ready to be adopted when they are 8 to 12 weeks old. If you want to add a beagle to your family, find a reputable **breeder**. A good breeder will make sure the puppy is healthy and has had its shots.

Beagle puppies learn quickly. It is important to begin **socializing** your new family member right away. Over time, introduce your puppy to new people and surroundings. Allowing the dog to make friends will make it a happier pet. Beagles make loyal family members for 12 to 15 years.

A litter of beagle puppies can range from only 2 to as many as 14!

Glossary

American Kennel Club (AKC) - an organization that studies and promotes interest in purebred dogs.

breed - a group of animals sharing the same ancestors and appearance. A breeder is a person who raises animals. Raising animals is often called breeding them.

Canidae (KAN-uh-dee) - the scientific Latin name for the dog family. Members of this family are called canids. They include wolves, jackals, foxes, coyotes, and domestic dogs.

civil war - a war between groups in the same country. The United States of America and the Confederate States of America fought a civil war from 1861 to 1865.

dense - thick or compact.

hazel - a color that combines brown, green, and gray.

lemon - a shade of tan that is so light it appears to be yellow.

litter - all of the puppies born at one time to a mother dog.

merge - to combine or blend.

microchip - an electronic circuit placed under an animal's skin. A microchip contains identifying information that can be read by a scanner.

muzzle - an animal's nose and jaws.

neuter (NOO-tuhr) - to remove a male animal's reproductive glands.

nutrient - a substance found in food and used in the body. It promotes growth, maintenance, and repair.

pregnant - having one or more babies growing within the body.

shed - to cast off hair, feathers, skin, or other coverings or parts by a natural process.

socialize - to adapt an animal to behaving properly around people or other animals in various settings.

spay - to remove a female animal's reproductive organs.

tricolor - having three colors.

undercoat - short hair or fur partly covered by longer protective fur.

vaccine (vak-SEEN) - a shot given to prevent illness or disease.

Websites

To learn more about Dogs, visit **booklinks.abdopublishing.com**. These links are routinely monitored and updated to provide the most current information available.

Index